IMAGES
of England

NORTON

St James's church, the Elizabethan buildings of Norton Hall and the preaching cross in its original position, 1813. Even though there is speculation about a Saxon origin for a church in Norton, documentary evidence suggests that the oldest parts of the present building date from the late twelfth century, possibly around 1180. At this time the Lord of the Manor, Robert FitzRanulph, bestowed the church on the newly established Beauchief Abbey. The traditional story linking FitzRanulph to the murder in 1170 of Thomas à Becket, Archbishop of Canterbury, is a subject of dispute amongst historians.

The thirteenth, fourteenth and fifteenth centuries saw the north and south aisles added, the chancel enlarged, clerestory windows included and a porch built. All this would account for the peculiar architecture of the nave, which has octagonal pillars on the south, round pillars on the north side, one round arch to the south aisle and all the other arches pointed. The Blythe Chapel was built as a chantry in or about 1520 by Geoffrey Blythe, Bishop of Lichfield, in memory of his parents William and Saffery Blythe, whose effigies lie on the ornately carved tomb. The chapel was later used as a private burial place for some of the Lords of the Manor. Many further alterations were made in accordance with religious practices of the times. Evidence of such changes was swept away in the extensive restoration of the church in 1881-82. This was under the direction of George Edmund Street, the foremost ecclesiastical architect of his day, also responsible for the Law Courts in London. The galleries and box pews were removed as was the three-decker pulpit. The tower arch was opened up, the external door to the Blythe Chapel was blocked, the organ repositioned and the exterior steps to the west gallery were also removed. Most of the stained glass dates from this time. The churchyard, for many centuries the burial ground for a portion of North Derbyshire, was closed for burials in 1869. Since then it has been much altered by the removal of broken and defaced gravestones and by the levelling of the ground in 1960. The grave of Sir Frances Chantrey, marked by a huge but simple slab of granite, is near the porch. A small Garden of Rest, created in 1956 and based on the Easter Garden theme, incorporates a grindstone, recalling the former local industry of scythemaking. A stone's throw from a busy road, the area round the church is a haven of tranquillity, a place to pause and reflect.

IMAGES
of England

NORTON

Compiled by
Norton History Group

TEMPUS

First published 2000
Copyright © Norton History Group, 2000

Tempus Publishing Limited
The Mill, Brimscombe Port,
Stroud, Gloucestershire, GL5 2QG

ISBN 0 7524 2052 6

Typesetting and origination by
Tempus Publishing Limited
Printed in Great Britain by
Midway Clark Printing, Wiltshire

This rural local view is something of a mystery. The picture has been shown to many local residents but none has been able to identify it with certainty. Suggestions have included Graves Park, Hazelbarrow Lane, below Grange Farm and various other parts of the Moss Valley.

Contents

Dedication

We dedicate this book

to the memory of

Bernard W.N. Cooper and Ted Jessop

Past Presidents, Norton History Group.

Without their enthusiasm and local knowledge

this book would not have been written.

Introduction

When Harold Armitage published his book *Chantreyland* in 1910, he described Norton as a mainly rural community, going back over a thousand years. Little remains of the mediaeval hamlets of the old Derbyshire parish, which stretched from Herdings in the east, to Bradway in the west with the natural boundaries of the Moss Brook, Meers Brook and River Sheaf to the north and south.

The church alone stands sentinel to the passing of history since its foundation in 1180, when it was served by the monks of Beauchief Abbey. Sir Francis Chantrey chose its graveyard as his burial place. Born to a tenant farmer at Jordanthorpe in 1781, he attended the local Free School, was apprenticed in Sheffield, then took the turnpike to London, to find fame and fortune as the foremost sculptor of his time. Today many of his works still grace some of the country's most illustrious buildings.

Norton has never been a quiet backwater. It has made a rich contribution to history in the two Blythe brothers who became bishops, Leonard Gill who founded Norton Free School in 1654, the exploits in Canada of the Kirkes of Greenhill and the stories of the influential Bagshawe, Offley and Shore families. The steel magnate Charles Cammell bought the Norton Hall Estate in 1852 and other land in the area.

Now Norton is mainly in South Yorkshire, although many of the wide vistas enjoyed by residents reach out into Derbyshire and the Peak District. New parishes have been carved from the old; large houses have been demolished or converted to other use but there are still small working farms. The lanes have been superseded by wide roads, the old tram from Sheffield via Woodseats to Meadowhead replaced by the new Supertram via Gleadless to a terminus at Herdings. As the number of houses in Norton has increased, so the provision of educational establishments has also diversified and now caters for all ages.

We trust this collection of photographs will give pleasure to many people who fondly remember the 'old Norton', whose forebears lived here and fashioned the way of life that has almost disappeared. Norton has been absorbed by Sheffield but its rural origins can still be enjoyed and its history traced. Norton is a little treasure whose heritage we should value.

Acknowledgements

We extend our grateful thanks to the many people who have allowed us to use their photographs, either the originals or copies, and to those who have borrowed treasured photographs from older family members and friends.

Other people have given permission for us to use copyright material and have supplied us with information for the captions. We thank them, especially D. Hindmarch and his colleagues in the Local Studies Library, Sheffield Libraries, Archives and Information; J. MacDonald, Archivist, The Cutlers' Company of Hallamshire; Norton Free School; Norton Woodseats Cricket Club; St James's Church Archive; Seaman Photographer Ltd; Sheffield Local Education Authority; Sheffield Newspapers Ltd; H. Tempest.

We hope that the following list does not omit any names but if yours is not included, please accept our apologies. Some names are of people who have died recently whose contributions we wish to acknowledge.

G.C. Aitcheson, P. Archer, J. Barnes, A. Biglands, M. Binney, N. Binney, J. Brackenbury, G.D. Brooks, H. Clayton, W.H. Coombs, B.W.N. Cooper, D. Coyle, M. Crookes, V. Crann, F. Creaser, J. Cutler, R. de Mercado, Mrs Deprez, P. Elinskas, J. Elliott, Mrs Finlay, M. Gascoigne, F.N. Gibbs, P. Haddock, V. and J. Harris, D. Harrison, W.J. Izzard, E. Jessop, S.R. Jones, P. Knutton, G. Linley, J. McGurk, G. Middleton, J. Mitchell, E. Parkin, L. Platts, M. Ponton, D. Powell, E. Purnell, D. Ridgway, D. Robinson, J. Robinson, P. and B. Rothwell, W. Ryals, Mrs Senior, A.R. Shaw, Mrs Shaw, N. Simpson, A.V. Smith, H.W. Smith, G. South, R. Stevens, G. Styring, B. Symonds, S. and K. Thompson, K. Thornton, Mr Unwin, J. Waller, S. Wetherill, J. Wheldon, Mrs White, J. Widdowson, W. Wild, N. Wragg, D. Wright.

This book has been compiled by: Michael Bland, Pamela Bower, Sheila Gilmour, Alan Hill, Joy Phillips, Anne Phipps, Kathryn Simpson, Margaret Turley, Peggy Vardy and Margaret Wilmott, members of Norton History Group.

One
O Come All Ye Faithful

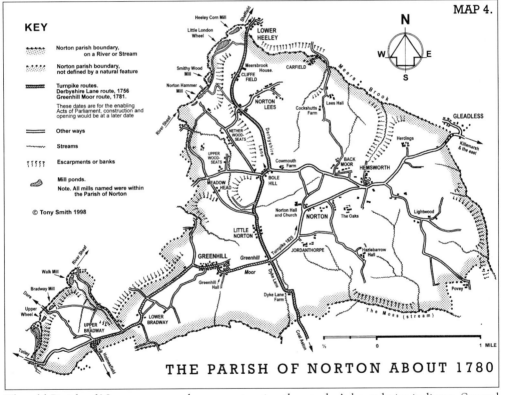

KEY

- Norton parish boundary, on a River or Stream
- Norton parish boundary, not defined by a natural feature
- Turnpike routes. Derbyshire Lane route, 1756 Greenhill Moor route, 1781.
  These dates are for the enabling Acts of Parliament, construction and opening would be at a later date
- Other ways
- Streams
- Escarpments or banks
- Mill ponds.
  Note. All mills named were within the Parish of Norton

© Tony Smith 1998

MAP 4.

THE PARISH OF NORTON ABOUT 1780

The old Parish of Norton was much more extensive than today's boundaries indicate. Several changes, both political and ecclesiastical, have carved up the area into the suburbs of Bradway, Greenhill, Meersbrook, Norton Lees, Woodseats and parts of Gleadless and Heeley. Norton is now the area within a radius of approximately one mile of St James's church and includes Batemoor and Jordanthorpe. More poetically, it is sometimes referred to as Chantreyland, coined by Harold Armitage for his book on the district, a title which was inspired by Norton's most famous son, the sculptor Sir Frances Chantrey RA. The mediæval parish church has remained at the heart of Norton whilst other places of worship have developed in the surrounding suburbs.

The parish church of St James, Norton, around 1880, showing the exterior steps beside the main door, leading to the tower and west gallery. The wide gate allowed the entry of a bier. It was replaced when the whole gateway was re-designed in 1968.

The Bullock Memorial commemorates William Bullock, Lord of the Manor, a keen supporter of the Royalist cause. His estates were sequestered during Oliver Cromwell's Long Parliament and restored to him on the accession of Charles II. William died in 1666 and his only son, John, died from smallpox in 1682, aged nineteen.

Interior of St James's, pre-1906, with corona lights and brass lectern. The altar shows a ridel curtain behind, together with oak panelling. Later removal of the curtain revealed the east window, a gift from Bernard Cammell in memory of his father, Charles. The oak panelling was removed and part of it re-carved, by Advent Hunstone of Tideswell, to form a screen in the North aisle.

Interior, Blythe chapel, St James's, showing the reredos installed in 1920. This was designed by Advent Hunstone, given by his brother Ernest Hunstone of Park Farm, Little Norton, and later removed to the Rector's Vestry. The credence table was donated by Revd G.W. Hall and the hand-carved communion rails by Miss Gladys Bagshawe. Cornelius Clarke, Lord of the Manor, who died in 1694, is remembered by a stone wall-tablet to the right of the altar.

Choirboys of St James's church, photographed by Revd G.W. Hall, vicar from 1888 to 1926. The font dates from around 1220 and the curtain in the background was used as the bell-tower screen until 1969.

The Shaw brothers, who were in Norton church choir, won a Five Trebles singing competition in 1897. From left to right: Walter, aged ten, Bertrand, aged sixteen, Stanley, aged eight, Arthur, aged fourteen, William, aged twelve. Bertrand (Bert) Shaw became parish clerk after the death of his father in 1929 and held the post of verger until 1951. He is remembered for his prompt attention to smoking oil lamps during services!

To Commemorate
the First Broadcast Service
from Norton Parish Church,
on Sunday, January, the 17th
.1954.

Preacher: The Rev. Leonard Schiff of the United Theological College, Bangalore, South India. The Service (which included portions of the liturgy of the Church of South India) was conducted by the Rev. Rolf Gledhill, the Rector of Norton.

Members of the Choir.

Boys.			Men.
G. Maynard.	B. Marshall.	Alto:-	C.A.Gordon.
H.Marshall.	I. King.	J. Randall.	D.B.Allen.
G. King.	I. Macdonald.	Tenor:-	H. Tow.
G. Fitton.	C. Barnes.	J.A. Allen.	W.H.J.Coombs
R.Pitchfork.	J. Beckett.	Bass:-	
A. Bower.	D. Arnold.	F. M Barden.	B.B.Wilkinson.
A. Vardy.	I. Smith.	R. L Jones.	H. Hoddinott.

J. Allen.
Organist and Choirmaster.

F. M. Darlow.
C. A. Gordon.
Church wardens.

Rev. Rolf Gledhill. M.A. B.D.
Rector of Norton.
Rural Dean of Stavely.

Details of the Broadcast Service from Norton Parish Church on 17 January 1954.

The remains of the old preaching cross, St James's churchyard, Norton. It is a Grade II listed monument and of fourteenth-century origin. Previously sited near the west wall of the churchyard, it was moved in order to accommodate the grave of Sir Francis Chantrey, who died in 1841.

The mysterious doorway, south side, St James's church, Norton. Its external existence was revealed in 1943, when the ivy covering the wall was blown down in a storm. Even though plaster covering the inside walls of the church has now been removed, it is still difficult to trace the outline of this door. Several suggestions have been put forward for its existence. It may have been the priest's entrance to the chancel, used in pre-reformation times, or the entrance to the vaults, which are now sealed.

Norton Church Bell Ringers, winners of the Old East Derbyshire Change Ringers' Challenge Cup, 1898. From left to right: J. Atkin, T.G. Sarel, J. Allen (conductor), W. Biggin, A. Slater, E. James.

Unveiling of Norton War Memorial, 26 June 1920, by Mrs Isherwood-Bagshawe of Norton Oakes. The memorial was erected by public subscription in memory of the fallen of the 1914-1918 war. A further stone was added in 1999 to commemorate those who died in the 1939-1945 war and subsequent conflicts.

The stone horse trough bearing the inscription: 'To the memory of Annie Hall of Norton Vicarage. Erected by parishioners and other friends. AD 1905.' Originally this was sited at the junction of Blackstock and Hemsworth Roads as a watering place to refresh weary horses after the long haul from the city. It was re-positioned near the Chantrey Monument in 1956, when the new traffic island was made. Mrs Hall was greatly concerned for the welfare of all animals and an interesting feature of the horse trough is an additional drinking bowl for dogs.

The earliest recorded gravestone in St James's churchyard, Norton. The churchyard was closed for burials in May 1869, after which burials took place at the Derbyshire Lane Cemetery, often referred to as Norton Cemetery.

The Chantrey Monument, Norton, erected in 1854, was designed by Philip Hardwick, RA, an old friend of Chantrey. It consists of a solid piece of Cheeswring granite, 22ft high, which was brought by sea from Cornwall to Hull and then by road to Norton. Norton House can be seen in the background, showing boundary railings.

A flock of sheep outside Norton Vicarage, 1900. The obelisk in the foreground was erected in memory of Sir Francis Chantrey, sculptor, who died in 1841.

Laying the foundation stones of the Church Hall, St James's, Norton, 16 September 1950. One of the eight stones was laid by Revd R. Gledhill. The picture also shows the cruck barn which was part of the Norton House stable block, demolished in 1960.

The opening of Norton Church Hall, 2 June 1951, by Bishop Rawlinson, Lord Bishop of Derby. The Revd Rolf Gledhill is seated on the Bishop's left.

The opening ceremony of Bradway Hall Church on 26 January 1952 was conducted by the clergy, from right to left: The Archdeacon of Chesterfield, Revd R. Gledhill (Rector of Norton), Revd T. M.Archer (Rural Dean of Eyam), Revd B.D. Cornish. The Norton churchwardens Messrs G.A. Wilkinson and F. Wynne-Jones, Mr and Mrs A.L. Beckett, Mrs Wynne-Jones and Mrs Lockwood complete the group.

The Lord Bishop of Derby, the two Archdeacons, the clergy, choir and part of the congregation at the dedication of the Church Hall of St Peter, Greenhill, on 13 November 1954. The building was made possible by local efforts and generous grants.

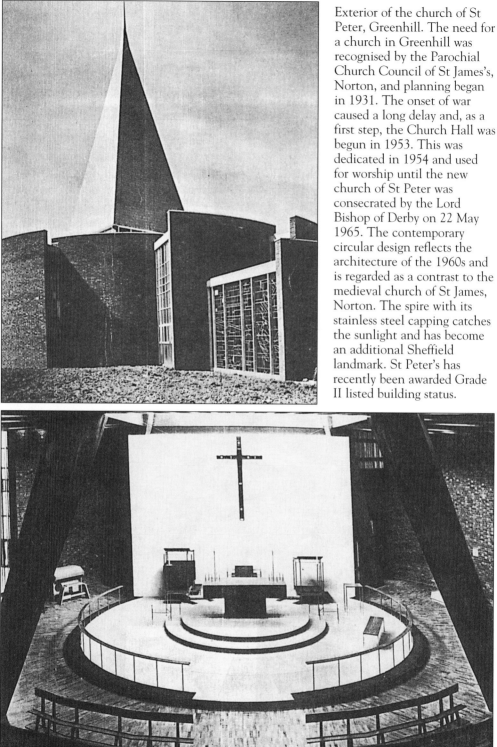

Exterior of the church of St Peter, Greenhill. The need for a church in Greenhill was recognised by the Parochial Church Council of St James's, Norton, and planning began in 1931. The onset of war caused a long delay and, as a first step, the Church Hall was begun in 1953. This was dedicated in 1954 and used for worship until the new church of St Peter was consecrated by the Lord Bishop of Derby on 22 May 1965. The contemporary circular design reflects the architecture of the 1960s and is regarded as a contrast to the medieval church of St James, Norton. The spire with its stainless steel capping catches the sunlight and has become an additional Sheffield landmark. St Peter's has recently been awarded Grade II listed building status.

Interior of the church of St Peter, Greenhill, showing the circular sanctuary area.

After the construction of the Gleadless Valley estate in the 1950s, St John the Evangelist church was dedicated in December 1960. The building itself was multi-purpose, with the altar area closed off during social activities. The Revd C.R. George, curate of Norton, was priest-in-charge of St John's and lived in Orpen Drive until the parish house was completed in late 1960.

After the Revd George's final service in October 1964, the congregation gathered for a group photograph. Amongst other organisations attached to the church were the Church Lads' Brigade, the Girls' Life Brigade, the Brownies and the Women's Fellowship. St John's closed for worship in April 1999.

Holy Grove chapel was built on land at Hemsworth Road, Norton Backmoor, bought in 1852 by T.B. Holy of Norton House. It opened as a Wesleyan Reform chapel in 1854. In 1876 the widowed Mrs Holy sold the land back to Charles Cammell. Many of the congregation had moved to the newly-built Mount View. Primitive Methodists leased the chapel in 1877 and bought it in 1887. The New Inn can be seen along the road.

Mrs Gladys Styring was born in the house at Hemsworth Road chapel. Her father, Mr John Bell, was the chapel keeper from 1911-1913. In 1936, after a case of diphtheria in the caretaker's family, the congregation was ordered to put in modern drainage. The Circuit Commission felt the cost too great and the chapel was sold. A house now stands on the site, almost opposite Matthews Lane.

Two

The Rich Man in his Castle

Norton Hall from the Deer Park, a view included in the Estate Sale plan of 1850. The sale followed the failure of the Parker-Shore Bank in 1843, ending the long ownership by the Offley and Shore families. The Hall was purchased in 1852 by Mr Charles Cammell, the steel magnate.

Norton Hall was owned for a few years by Mr W.F. Goodliffe, then purchased in 1905 by Mr B. Firth. The Cammell family had enlarged the Hall, adding the large oak-panelled room with a bay window and also the colonnade, used as an orangery. In 1916, Mr Firth allowed the Hall to be used by Royal Flying Corps officers. It was seldom used after the war but events such as Woodseats Baptist church summer fête were held in the grounds.

The less-often seen eastern side of Norton Hall in 1994. The Hall was sold in 1925 and became, in turn, the Firth Auxiliary Hospital, the Jessop Hospital Norton Annexe and then Beechwood, a private hospital. The nurses were proud of the connection between the Hall and Florence Nightingale, a member of the Shore family who lived here in the past. After several years of neglect it is now being renovated to form private dwellings.

Charles Cammell, one of the pioneers of modern industrial Sheffield, was born in Hull in 1810 and began his working life as apprentice to an ironmonger. He came to Sheffield about 1830 and started as a steel manufacturer in a very small way. His business grew and developed until he was the head of one of the world's largest steel works. It was in 1857 that he bought Norton Hall. This picture represents a fête that was held in the grounds of Norton Hall on August 4th 1860, to celebrate Mr Cammell's fiftieth birthday. The guests, who were the workpeople and their families, numbered over three thousand. The workmen walked in procession from Sheffield but conveyances were provided for the women and children. Dinner was served in a vast marquee and it seems to have been on a liberal scale. At all events, a contemporary account says: 'There were served up at the dinner two bullocks, four sheep, twenty eight lambs, four calves, sixty hams, two hundred and fifty plum puddings, ducks and fowls innumerable, five hundred four-pound loaves, buns, cake, wine and forty four, thirty-six gallon barrels of beer.' The workpeople presented the master with a massive gold plate candelabrum valued at five hundred guineas. After dinner there were sports for prizes given by Mr Cammell, archery, sack-racing, and bands of music for dancing. (*Sheffield Daily Telegraph* 1937)

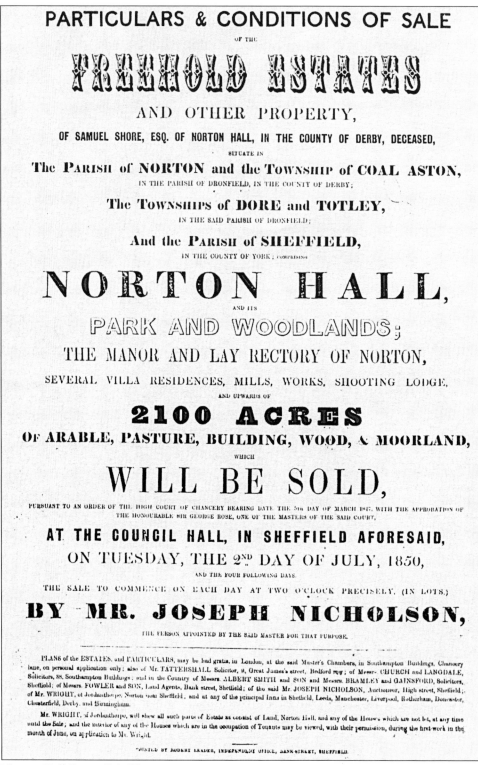

PARTICULARS & CONDITIONS OF SALE

OF THE

FREEHOLD ESTATES

AND OTHER PROPERTY,

OF SAMUEL SHORE, ESQ. OF NORTON HALL, IN THE COUNTY OF DERBY, DECEASED,

SITUATE IN

The PARISH of NORTON and the TOWNSHIP of COAL ASTON,

IN THE PARISH OF DRONFIELD, IN THE COUNTY OF DERBY;

The TOWNSHIPS of DORE and TOTLEY,

IN THE SAID PARISH OF DRONFIELD;

And the PARISH of SHEFFIELD,

IN THE COUNTY OF YORK; COMPRISING

NORTON HALL,

AND ITS

PARK AND WOODLANDS;

THE MANOR AND LAY RECTORY OF NORTON,

SEVERAL VILLA RESIDENCES, MILLS, WORKS, SHOOTING LODGE,

AND UPWARDS OF

2100 ACRES

OF ARABLE, PASTURE, BUILDING, WOOD, & MOORLAND,

WHICH

WILL BE SOLD,

PURSUANT TO AN ORDER OF THE HIGH COURT OF CHANCERY BEARING DATE THE 5TH DAY OF MARCH 1847, WITH THE APPROBATION OF
THE HONOURABLE SIR GEORGE ROSE, ONE OF THE MASTERS OF THE SAID COURT,

AT THE COUNCIL HALL, IN SHEFFIELD AFORESAID,

ON TUESDAY, THE 2ND DAY OF JULY, 1850,

AND THE FOUR FOLLOWING DAYS.

THE SALE TO COMMENCE ON EACH DAY AT TWO O'CLOCK PRECISELY, (IN LOTS,)

BY MR. JOSEPH NICHOLSON,

THE PERSON APPOINTED BY THE SAID MASTER FOR THAT PURPOSE.

PLANS of the ESTATES, and PARTICULARS, may be had gratis, in London, at the said Master's Chambers, in Southampton Buildings, Chancery lane, on personal application only; also of Mr. TATTERSHALL Solicitor, 9, Great James's street, Bedford row; of Messrs. CHURCH and LANGDALE, Solicitors, 88, Southampton Buildings; and in the Country of Messrs. ALBERT SMITH and SON and Messrs. BRAMLEY and GAINSFORD, Solicitors, Sheffield; of Messrs. FOWLER and SON, Land Agents, Bank street, Sheffield; of the said Mr. JOSEPH NICHOLSON, Auctioneer, High street, Sheffield; of Mr. WRIGHT, of Jordanthorpe, Norton near Sheffield, and at any of the principal Inns in Sheffield, Leeds, Manchester, Liverpool, Rotherham, Doncaster, Chesterfield, Derby, and Birmingham.

Mr. WRIGHT, of Jordanthorpe, will shew all such parts of Estate as consist of Land, Norton Hall, and any of the Houses which are not let, at any time until the Sale; and the interior of any of the Houses which are in the occupation of Tenants may be viewed, with their permission, during the first week in the month of June, on application to Mr. Wright.

PRINTED BY ROBERT LEADER, INDEPENDENT OFFICE, BANK-STREET, SHEFFIELD.

Norton Hall Estate Sale Plan.

Mrs Muriel Isherwood-Bagshawe of Norton Oakes and Sister Mary O'Neill of Norton Hall, which was then the Norton Annexe of Jessop Hospital.

A small group of nurses on the lawn at Norton Hall Annexe, 1948. Students from the United Sheffield hospitals worked here for a few weeks during their training in order to gain experience in gynaecological care. Student nurse Janet Coy (Mrs F. McGurk) on the right, back row, later came to live in Norton.

Maids on the roof at Norton Hall, dressing up and having fun in their spare time. One of these, or the photographer, was Nora Ashton, later Mrs Jackson.

The Norton Colony was formed in 1896 by a group of idealistic young men who wished to lead a simple, self-sufficient life in a community. Hugh Mapleton was a founder member and his surname can still be seen on products in health food shops. The men lived in the present Nursery Lodge and used the walled garden of Norton Hall and its five greenhouses to grow fruit and vegetables. The group was closely linked with Edward Carpenter and the Sheffield Socialists.

The ancient surnames of Parker and Gill are linked with the Oakes-in-Norton in the sixteenth and seventeenth centuries. Elizabeth Gill married Richard Bagshawe in 1721 and the Bagshawe family, one of the oldest in Derbyshire, remained at the Oakes until 1984. The cedar tree was planted in 1770 and much of the design of the garden dates from this period.

The gardens of the Oakes are listed in the National Register of Parks and Gardens of Special Historic Interest in England. In the early nineteenth century the house was re-modelled and the garden to the west side was replanted, including the magnolia seen near the house. The front terrace and urns were designed by Sir Francis Chantrey and set up in 1838, making a fine foreground to the Doric portico.

Mr John Ponton (left) with Mr Isherwood-Bagshawe by the front terrace at Norton Oakes, giving a closer view of one of the Chantrey urns.

(C RICHARDSON NEWSAGENT) No. 16 .
ENTRANCE TO GARDENS, BAGSHAW PARK

The early eighteenth-century garden gates at the Oakes are Grade II* listed. The elaborate wrought iron gates are thought to have been made locally from metal obtained on the estate.

Children playing outside the Oakes Lodge on School Lane, Norton. The high wall enclosing Norton Green's garden is on the right.

School Lane, Norton, in the 1950s, showing the entrance to the old post office yard on the left, and the garden and buildings of Norton Green on the right.

Col. Nathaniel Creswick resided at Chantrey Grange in the 1890s and shortly afterwards changed the house name to Norton Green. Norton Green, the Maugerhay cottages and Spring House were all demolished in 1974. They were replaced by the Northern Counties Housing Association flats.

This land was formerly the ancient Norton bowling green. Parties of people came from Sheffield to play bowls and to take tea in the old stone Bowling Green House. This was bought by James Addy in 1866, rebuilt, enlarged and renamed as Chantrey Grange.

This fine carved oak mantelpiece bears the date 1623 and the initials L.G., indicating the date of the first Jacobean Norton House and the name of its owner, Leonard Gill. When the House was demolished in 1878 the fireplace was taken to Derwent Hall in Derbyshire. Then, when that house was sold in 1927, it was presented to The Cutlers' Company, a very apt gift because it was contemporaneous with the founding of the Company in 1624.

Norton House in the 1920s. It was built for Bernard Cammell but by the time it was finished in 1880 he had inherited Norton Hall. Mr E.M.E. Welby, Stipendiary Magistrate of Sheffield, rented it from 1881 to about 1916. It was sold in 1927 to M.J. Gleeson, builder. Norton House was used by the Home Guard during the Second World War; some of them bought it after the war and founded the present Norton House Country Club.

A reminder of days when the daily milk was brought round in churns and dipped out in pint measures. The central part of the Vicarage, next to the horse and cart, was built between 1714 and 1718 by the Revd Cavendish Nevile, using his considerable personal fortune, and five years later he added the elegant library at the north end. In 1902, the large parish dining room was added on at the south side.

An unusual view from the church tower showing the Vicarage, the green, the Chantrey memorial and Norton House, possibly around 1920.

The Revd G.W. Hall's wife, Annie (née Gladwin), standing at the front entrance of the Rectory on Norton Church Road. Gardening was one of her favourite hobbies.

Maids at the Rectory during the Revd G.W. Hall's ministry, 1888-1929.

The Revd John Stanton Pegge, Rector of Norton 1929-1944, Mrs Pegge, Eleanor, Richard and Veronica. All three children served their country in the Second World War, Eleanor and Veronica as nurses in South Africa, Richard in the Army.

Richard Pegge in the front garden of the Rectory, home on leave from the Army. He was a 2nd Lt in the York and Lancaster Regiment and served with much gallantry before being killed in action in Tobruk in 1941, aged twenty-seven.

The Old Rectory in 1928 showing part of the extensive garden which then included the area now occupied by the new Rectory. The door on the right led to the room containing the parish library, so avoiding the necessity of readers having to pass through the house.

In the library is a wall moulding of a medallion portrait of Sir Francis Chantrey by Heffernan, who was Chantrey's assistant for thirty years. The coat of arms above it is of the Nevile family. The Revd Cavendish Nevile came to Norton in 1710 and established a superb parish library of scholarly books, mostly of theology and science. The collection is now housed at the Sheffield University Library.

The Grange was built in 1744 for Mr Lowe, the Non-Conformist minister to the Offley family of Norton Hall. A later minister, the Revd Henry Piper, ran a boys' boarding school here from 1814 to 1833. The Grange was sold in 1850 and for a while was called Hill Top. Later occupants included Mr William Fisher, JP and Mr John Gladwin, whose daughter Annie married the Revd G.W. Hall, Vicar of Norton.

A photograph taken at Norton Grange, the family home of the Gladwins, possibly of the gardener.

The Chantry cottage was given listed building status in 1969. It was built towards the end of the eighteenth century, probably as part of the improvement of Norton Hall and its estate. Use was made of old seventeenth-century timbers for the ceiling joists. There is a long tradition that a chantry priest, established by the Blythe family in 1524, lived on or near this site. There are references in the parish registers to families at the Chantry from 1654 to 1741.

The gales of February 1962 wrought havoc throughout Sheffield. Many fine trees bordering the bend of Norton Lane near Chantry Cottage and Norton House Country Club fell across the road.

Mr G.A. Widdowson in the long lean-to greenhouse in the nursery of H.D. Widdowson & Son on Norton Lane, formerly the walled garden of Norton Hall. Father and son were at Norton from 1929 to 1939 and are famous for producing the first apricot-coloured Viola, named Chantreyland, still found in gardens today.

The Sheffield Parks Department took over the Nursery in 1939 and this is a happy reminder of the crowds which flocked to Norton Nursery Open Days in the 1960s and 1970s. Practical demonstrations took place and advice about gardening problems could be obtained. The greenhouses were filled with plants grown to a very high standard, later to be planted in the parks and in floral decorations throughout the city. Floral displays were entered at major horticultural shows.

The water leaving the boating lake in Graves Park falls through a short but steep ravine. Steps, seen here during a dry spell in the 1930s, were built into the stream to form a cascade.

The cascade, or waterfall, in full spate.

The Summer House of Norton Hall was a substantial stone building furnished in style, according to a Norton lady who also remembered the polished wooden floors strewn with animal skin rugs, around the time of the First World War. From 1950 it became semi-derelict and in 1967 it was declared unsafe and demolished.

Graves Park, formerly the grounds of Norton Hall, was opened to the public in June 1926. The first pavilion and tea room was erected in April 1927, not far from the Summer House. Its popularity probably grew after the provision of toilets in 1929!

This was the coach house in Summer House Wood, Graves Park. The carriages were not used by the family at Norton Hall but by the occupants of the Summer House, which can be glimpsed at the top of the slope above. Now, when walking along the path leading from the Bolehill Lodge towards the café, there is only a slight depression in the grass on the left to indicate the site of the pond in front of the coach house.

Gentlemen in Graves Park, date unknown. Suggestions regarding their occupation include an army officer, chauffeur, policeman and park keeper.

Jordanthorpe House in 1967 was set well back from Norton Lane. The grounds to the north are now covered by a huge traffic roundabout and dual carriageway. Jordanthorpe is a location named in various wills and documents dating from the 1500s.

Three
The Poor Man at his Gate

The Maxey family visiting relatives in Harvey Clough Road. This was the last house at the north-east end of the road, which then ended in a muddy track leading into Woodland Road. The Knutt family lived here for some forty years before it was demolished and flats built in the 1960s. A similar house can still be seen higher up Harvey Clough Road, on the opposite side.

The three groups of cottages on School Lane in 1957, not often seen together in one photograph. They are within the grounds of the Oakes but are usually referred to as part of Maugerhay hamlet.

A postcard posted in 1908 showing the post office yard with the schoolmaster's house to the left. Mr Atkin introduced gardening as a school activity in 1906 and some of the boys practised their skills in his garden! Note the pump in the foreground.

Two groups of cottages in School Lane, Norton, date not known. On the left was the post office and the homes of Mrs Rhodes and Mr and Mrs Ponton and two families lived on the right. It was usual to see someone gardening in the evenings. The cottages must have looked like this for at least a century, until they were sold in the 1970s and greatly altered inside.

The pair of cottages below the post office on School Lane in 1908. These have been altered slightly in recent years to form one house. Tommy Lee, the parish clerk and registrar, lived on one side in 1881 and his son Fred and family on the other.

Cottages 1-4 Maugerhay in 1906. These were at right angles to the present Chantrey House, whose chimneys can be seen in the centre. They were dismantled in 1971 and rebuilt in the same style to form a wing of the house, using the original stone. The rooks nesting in the distant trees have transferred their activities to the large sycamore tree on the left.

Chantrey (not Chantry) House seems to be a twentieth-century name for this house in Maugerhay. Mr Jenkin, formerly of Hazelbarrow, bought the house and the four attached cottages on the right in the Norton Hall Estate sale in 1850. Occupants this century include Mr J.W.W. Badger 1914-1930, dairyman Mr Haw until the early 1950s, then Mr Hanwell 1959-1989, who carefully restored the main house.

A footpath from Matthews Lane and Norton Free School to Norton Lane, 1945. The chimneys of Spring House and Maugerhay show in the distance.

Maugerhay cottages behind Spring House, Norton Lane, in 1909. All that remains of this rural scene is the path from Norton Free School and the large tree on the left. Cottage No. 5 held a tiny shop at one time, selling sweets, sugar, tea, candles, paraffin and other basic goods.

Spring House was built by Mr Gascoigne soon after 1850. In 1900 it was bought by Mr Fielding, then landlord of the Bagshawe Arms. After his death in 1911 his family kept a shop there, also running Norton Post Office from 1939 to 1945. The cottages to the west side of Maugerhay can be seen at the back. They, with Spring House, were demolished in 1974 by the Northern Counties Housing Association and flats built.

Part of the large garden of Spring House, possibly in the early 1920s. The car belonged to Mr Hartley, son-in-law of Mr Fielding. Mrs Hartley, and later her daughter Mrs Allen, ran a shop and tea-room in the front rooms of the house. The Goff and then the Applegate families kept the shop until it closed in the 1970s. Behind the greenhouse a track ran from Norton Lane to Norton House Farm Cottage, seen on the left.

Nos 25-29 Ashbury Lane, Backmoor, shown on the 1804 enclosure map as two separate houses, two gardens and a croft, owned and tenanted by Joseph Ashbury.

No. 25 Ashbury Lane, Backmoor, was a typical nail maker's cottage of the eighteenth century. It once had an anvil, known locally as a stithy, in the then workshop on the left of the house. The stithy was broken up and used to help fill in the well, the site of which is now marked by the apple tree.

William Archer's house on Mawfa Lane taken in 1973, shortly before it was demolished. Mr Archer and his sons Leslie and Cyril were the local blacksmiths and wheelwrights. In their nearby workshops they shod horses, made carts and provided many a local coffin.

The Coupe family have lived at Ivy Cottage for some fifty years. For many years Mr Coupe kept poultry and sold eggs here but recently four houses were built in the garden. In a deed of 1863 the building is referred to as the Chantrey Arms. Perhaps it could not compete against the New Inn and Nailmakers' because soon afterwards it appears in the records as Grove Cottage.

Four Lane Ends, Norton Lees, showing the old Cross Scythes pub and cottages at the junction of Norton Lees Lane and Derbyshire Lane. The pub has the bay windows, the Newall family lived on the far side and the Misses Vickers on the right.

Cottages opposite the Cross Scythes, at the junction of Derbyshire Lane and Scarsdale Road (formerly Green Lane). They were perched somewhat precariously above the quarry and were so badly damaged in the storm of 1962 that they were demolished shortly afterwards. Two families lived here then; the Paramores were in the cottage on the left.

One row of these cottages in Little Norton survived until the 1960s. The families who lived here over the years had familiar Norton surnames such as Shaw, Biggin, Urton, Mather, Rhodes and Booker. Several worked at home as file cutters. Sarah Booker married Joseph Benson, who became Lord Mayor of Sheffield in 1920.

Painted Fabrics Meadow Head

The name in large letters on the workshop roof is that of Painted Fabrics Ltd. This company came to the First World War Women's Auxiliary Army Corps camp at Little Norton in 1923. The women's living quarters had been well built and provided homes and gardens for severely wounded ex-servicemen. The men, in spite of their terrible injuries, produced fabric and clothing of fine quality and design.

Old stone cottages in School Lane, Greenhill, about 1950, taken from the grounds of the school on the opposite corner. Greenfield Road houses can be seen beyond them. When the cottages were demolished in 1966, Greenfield Close was developed to replace them.

This stile leads to cottages at the back of Scott's Grange Farm, Greenhill, where three sisters of the Truelove family lived until the mid 1950s. Mrs Nellie Brown was in the stone-built part at the back of the farm in the corner, Sally lived in the centre and Annie Truelove at the School Lane end. Many people remember their brother and nephews working at the nearby forge, the Crabtree Works.

Stone Row and Brick Row, Bradway, photographed before 1910. Maps indicate that Stone Row was built some time between 1838 and 1875. The end bay of the school playground shelter can be seen just beyond. This, together with the Stone Row, was demolished in 1975 for road widening purposes. Brick Row was built in 1893 though the corner shop at the far end may have been built a little earlier, around 1886.

Midland Cottages, Bradway, in the early 1900s. A plaque on the front stated M.R.1876 so they were almost certainly built for Midland Railway or contractor staff while the tunnel was being made, 1865-1870. They were still occupied by a signalman and a platelayer in the 1930s. After demolition in the early 1960s a block of five shops was built on the site.

Four
Willingly To School

Moscar Wheel, Abbeydale, painted by W. Lowe in 1845. This was the first known cutlers' wheel on the River Sheaf. Rents from this property were left in trust by Leonard Gill, who died in 1654, to pay for a school master to give free education to fifteen poor children at Norton. Joseph Rodgers left Moscar Wheel in 1891 and it never worked again. Today only traces remain (see photographs in *Abbeydale and Millhouses* by P. Harvey, in this series).

The old school building in School Lane was rebuilt and enlarged in 1787 and demolished in 1953. The original school was founded in 1654 after Leonard Gill left a house and garden in Maugerhay in trust for this use for poor children of Norton. It is interesting to note that the original endowments provided education for girls as well as boys. It is named as Norton Free School in a will dated 1774.

Mr Joseph Atkin, the Headmaster, with staff and pupils in 1907 at Norton Free School, built on part of the Glebe land off Matthews Lane. Due to overcrowding on the School Lane site, this building was opened in 1895, incorporating the commemoration stone from the front of the old school.

Miss Ida Blanche Atkin's father, Joseph Atkin, was headmaster at Norton Free School for many years until his death in 1920. She took over from him but only for four years, as she died in 1924. During her short time in charge, she held the first Open Day for parents who 'showed great interest in the work in progress and the specimens exhibited'. She also took her staff to a physical training lecture and organised many visits for pupils, including a trip to the British Empire Exhibition at Wembley.

Some former staff of Norton Free School, from left to right: Miss Hilda Dungworth who left in 1946, Mr F.M. Barden, affectionately known as Billy, headmaster from 1941 to 1959, and Miss Alice Knowles.

Remains of air-raid shelter toilets at Norton Free School. This shelter, used from 1940 to 1945 and now sealed, was in the shape of a U with chemical toilets at either end. Wooden benches were provided for the children to sit on during air-raids.

The children from Norton Free School were taken to see the Barlow Hunt in 1960 when it met at the Oakes. A teacher, Mrs Bramhald, is at the back right with Miss Gwynedd Simons of Cloonmore Drive next to her.

Norton Free School children at the Barlow Hunt Meet at the Oakes between 1960 and 1965. The headmaster, Mr Walch, is at the back near the right. The onlookers are teachers, parents and other Norton people.

Norton Free School group about 1950, including Janet Goulson, Patricia Cartwick, Carol Shelton, Carol Watts and Tommy Martyn. The stone building on the right contained the outdoor toilets and sheds, demolished in 1963 as work to extend the school progressed. Note the two fields (now one) beside the gennel leading to Norton Lane.

A hot summer's day at Norton Free School in the 1940s or 1950s, when lessons were sometimes taken outside on the school field.

Julia Hole was crowned first May Queen of Norton Free School on 20 May 1947 by the sister in charge of the Jessop Hospital Annexe. During the celebrations there was singing and dancing by the children, who were accompanied by an orchestra formed by German prisoners of war from a nearby camp.

The tradition of appointing a May Queen at Norton Free School ended in 1970, when Frances Gilmour was crowned Queen Dianthus. From left to right: Diane Furness, infant teacher Mrs Walker, page boy Thomas Bell, Frances Gilmour, Helen Furness, Headmaster Mr Walch and Jane Green.

May Day celebrations at Norton Free School in 1950 or 1951. From left to right: Carole Watts, Sylvia Vardy, Patricia Cartwick, Margaret Beal, Pat Latham, Carol Shelton, Joan Hughes.

Norton Free School May Day revels in the Vicarage Field with the Grange in the background.

Norton Free School May Day revels in the Vicarage Field, *c.* 1960. The high wall is of Norton House kitchen garden.

This Norton Free reception class having fun on May Day 1967 is thought to be, from left to right: Jane Allonby, Julie Blagg, Wendy Adams, Suzanne Ackroyd, Angela Barron, one of the Battye twins in the chain mail, Jonathan Knowles, Alison Garlick, David Phillips, Nicholas Binney, Nicholas Frost, Michael Day in the helmet, Deborah Parkin, Philip Redford, Neil Moorhouse, Richard Gilson, Christopher Rothwell, David Bocking.

Junior 3/4, Norton Free School, in 1963. From left to right, back row: Sheila Guest, John Taunton, Barbara Smith, Elizabeth Kilburn, Barbara Purcell, Pamela Glover, Susan Jepson, Rosemary Bates, Frank Claypole, Robert Nicholls. Middle row: Patricia Robinson, Simon Ellis, David Lake, Michael Howard, Annette Stubbs, Pamela Ellis, Gillian Shepherd, Graham Shawcroft, Ian Jackson, Michael Hobdail, David Rogers, Jacqueline Plant. Front row: Nicholas Moore, Howard Waters, Caroline Wilkinson, Sheila Oldfield, Gail Ringstead, Janet Barber, Elizabeth Schofield, Elaine Manning, Nigel Hughes, Richard Ward.

PC Peter McGrath, Schools Liaison Officer, putting handcuffs on Jane Green during the 1968 Police Fortnight at Norton Free School. The other children include Susan Phillips, Andrew Iosson, Philip Harris, Andrew Gilmour, Suzanne Marsden, Andrew Meakin, Billy Marsden, Frances Gilmour, Diane Furniss, Martin Wilmott, Jane Pipes, Richard Storey and Neil Gray.

Gleadless Valley Secondary Modern School was opened in 1963. By the time it closed in 1996 it was a successful Comprehensive School but as pupil numbers fell it became increasingly difficult to remain viable. After demolition, the land was sold and the site is now occupied by a small private housing estate.

Alderman and Mrs Worrall at Jordanthorpe Secondary Modern School for Boys, greeted by Head Boy David Gibbs and Headmaster Mr Geoff Adams at the school speech day in 1962. Mr Adams was instrumental in establishing a reputation for hard work and success in examinations with pupils who had not passed the 11 plus test and was respected by pupils and staff. David Gibbs is now the Deputy Head at Mossbrook School.

The original educational establishment on this site was the Rowlinson Technical School, opened by HRH Princess Margaret in 1953. Rowlinson Campus was opened by the Rt Hon. Harold Wilson in 1971. David Sanderson, music teacher, is in the right foreground conducting an ensemble. The buildings were added to and now form the Norton Centre, part of Sheffield College.

The Chantrey and Oakes Park Schools in Matthews Lane were used for children with special needs. They opened in 1962, providing accommodation for 40 resident children and 140 day pupils, not only from Sheffield but also from adjoining areas. The schools have undergone several changes over the years and now the complex is known as Talbot School.

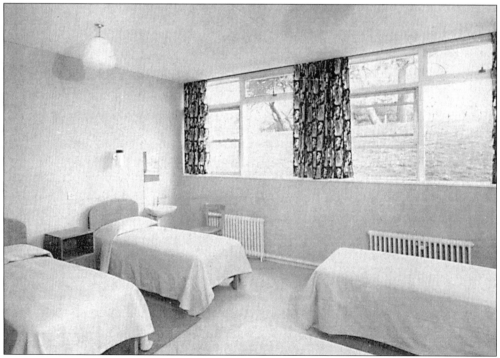

A former dormitory at Chantrey School.

Five

We Plough the Fields and Scatter

It is believed that an ancient farmhouse stood on this site at Herdings from the early 1300s. The families of Rollinson, Scriven, Jenkin, Hazard and Marsh have farmed here from the sixteenth century. This house has a 1675 date stone over the doorway. It became a Youth Club.

Oakes Farm Cottage off Mawfa Lane was a small holding with enough land for a few animals. Mr Fidler was there in 1920, moving on to farm at Carter Hall. The Bradbury family lived in the cottage for more than twenty years, leaving just before it was demolished in 1955. They grazed sheep in this field.

Mansion House Farm is Grade II listed. Made of stone with mullioned windows, it was probably built in the seventeenth century. Families at the farm since then have included Urton alias Steven, Atkin and Fox.

These old outbuildings at Haslehurst Farm are listed in an inventory of George Gill's property dated 1622.

Visiting Mrs Rose at Haslehurst Farm in 1983 are Mr Norman Darley, the Right Revd David Lunn, then Bishop of Sheffield and the Revd Mark Williams, then Rector of St James's, Norton.

This watercolour painting of Hazelbarrow Hall was owned by Mr Rhodes of the old Norton post office.

The Selioke tombstone in the Blythe Chapel in Norton church shows William Selioke, who died in 1541, and his wife Joyce. The earliest entries for Selioke in the parish registers, from 1562, record the baptism of children of George Selioke of Hazelbarrow, Gentleman. He died in 1577.

Traces of the old Hall can be seen to the left in this old photograph of Hazelbarrow Farm.

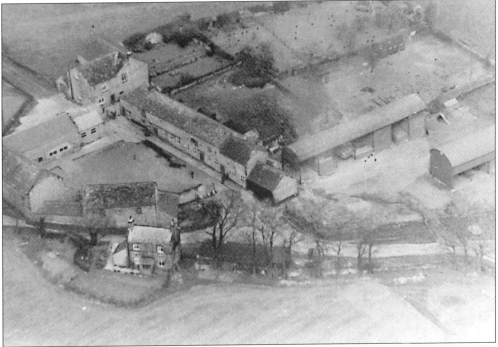

Demolition of the old Hall began on 10 May 1821. It was replaced by the present day Hazelbarrow farmhouse with its extensive outbuildings, old and new.

A welcome break during the Norton Ploughing Association match at Hazelbarrow Farm on 8 October 1948 with Win Swaffield of the Women's Land Army pouring tea for a lad from the Bagshawe Arms. Also in the group are Ron Gillott and Harold Glossop, smoking a pipe.

A technical hitch with the tractor, but a well-filled barn! TE-20 tractor and plough at Hazelbarrow Farm 1957.

Jordanthorpe Farm was rented by the Chantrey family from the Offley and later the Shore families of Norton Hall. Sir Francis Chantrey, RA, FRS, the sculptor, was born here on 7 April 1781. During the lifetime of his mother, Sir Francis had the house enlarged to its present size. It was a working farm until 1965, the last farmer being Mr Frank Shepherd.

A short distance from Meadow Head, along Little Norton Lane, was the entrance to Park Farm stackyard. Park Farm may well have been the early seventeenth-century home of John Parker, yeoman farmer and lead merchant of Little Norton.

Park Farm stackyard, a small gateway leading into the farm yard and the end of the outbuildings on the west side in 1935. Note the old lamp standard.

Mr Allen's horse and cart outside Park Farm, Little Norton, showing buildings on the west side of the yard in 1935. Mr Allen took over the farm from Mr Ernest Hunstone, his wife's uncle. Mr Hunstone was born in Tideswell but was at Park Farm for more than forty years. He died in 1932, so did not live to see the demolition of the farm in 1936.

Mr Allen leading a horse out into the yard at Park Farm. This ancient wing of the house extended to the left and was supported by cruck beams forming a number of bays. A large carved roof boss in the form of a rose was found when the house was taken down.

Mr Manby Allen driving cows from Park Farm back to the fields. The barns on the left and the pig farm and cottages seen here on the bend of Little Norton Lane were demolished in 1936-1937.

Mr Ernest Hunstone and his niece, Mrs Ethel Allen, in the farmyard at Park Farm, Little Norton, 1932. Hunstone Avenue at Meadowhead is named after him.

Mr Herbert Goy was a pig breeder and in 1931 he had a pig farm at 29 Little Norton Lane, across the gennel from Park Farm. Further along towards Norton Lane was Norton Woodseats football ground.

The central section of Greenhill Hall dated from the fourteenth century. Several well-known local families were connected with the Hall in the sixteenth century, including Jerome Blythe, Thurstan Kirke and John Bullock. Three grandsons of Thurstan Kirke played an important part in the early English colonization of Canada.

The Oak Room on the south side of Greenhill Hall, the entrance hall and two upper rooms were added by the Bullock family, who lived in the Hall from 1586. Their coat of arms is on the central panel of the fireplace.

The greater part of Greenhill Hall was built in the sixteenth century with an addition by John Lupton in the nineteenth century. This beautiful residence, then owned by Sheffield Corporation, sadly was demolished in 1965.

In 1900 Greenhill Hall and Farm were purchased by Mr James Andrew, whose name is commemorated in the nearby Crescent. Mr Levi Elliott moved there in 1934 and maintained a working farm until 1956.

Six
Serving the Community

The first Norton postman, John Witheford, lived in a cottage in the walled garden of Norton Hall. Herbert Rhodes of Backmoor married Ann Witheford in 1852 and took over as Rural Messenger when his father-in-law died in 1854. At that time Herbert and Ann were living in this cottage in School Lane so it became the Norton post office and stayed as such for the next eighty-five years. Business was transacted through the window.

Herbert Rhodes, by now the respected sub-post master, outside the post office and cottage in School Lane, Norton. Herbert also carried out the duties of School Board attendance officer. He died in November 1919, aged ninety-three, and was buried in Norton Cemetery.

Selina, the second wife of Herbert Rhodes, kept the post office in School Lane from 1919 until 1939 when the volume of mail generated at the beginning of the Second World War proved too much for her. Their daughter, Mabel, married John Ponton of Woodseats in October 1923 and lived in the cottage adjoining the post office. Mabel lived in Norton for most of her ninety-seven years and died in May 1991.

This view of the Bagshawe Arms was taken in the first few years of the twentieth century, when Fred Cuzner had taken over from Mr Fielding.

The landlord of the Bagshawe Arms, by now Mr Herbert Skelton, may be among this group of men but none of them has been named so far. The man in the centre looks as if he is wearing bicycle clips. The poster may be advertising Norton Agricultural Show, which was usually held in the field over the road in the 1930s.

Joe Wheldon Snr, wife Sarah and son Joe outside Wheldon's shop, Backmoor. An unnamed lady is at the entrance to the yard and storage barns situated on the west side of the house. This house is marked as Backmoor House on the 1906 Ordnance Survey map and so may be the same one noted in the records where a Mr Hawksmore lived in 1732.

Joe Wheldon Jnr, born 1887, is standing second from the left and two employees are on the right in this photograph. Young Joe delivered goods to Gleadless on his own when only twelve years old. The shop sold everything from pins to coal. The lamp standard here is not in earlier or later views.

Horse and cart outside Joe Wheldon's shop at Backmoor Road, Norton. It shows Sarah, wife of Joe Wheldon Snr, who is the man wearing the bowler hat; between them is Joe Wheldon Jnr. The man in the cart must be a customer.

Mr William Wheldon and his wife Bessie took over in about 1920. Joe Wheldon was mainly a corn factor, dealing with farmers, but the family built up the business into a good grocery and provisions shop.

Mrs Daisy Powell was very surprised when her husband bought the shop as her birthday present in 1936. He said her Mum, who lived with them, could look after the baby and the house. She ran the shop primarily as a grocery but sold many other items.

Mr Leslie Powell died in the early 1940s so the shop provided a livelihood for his family. It was hard work, from seven o'clock each morning. Daisy cooked ham and made cakes and children called on the way to school to order an apple pie on a plate to collect on the way home. The new shops on Constable Road caused trade to drop off and the shop closed in 1972.

This photograph dates from the late 1920s and shows how the New Inn at Backmoor looked in 1910 when local children could buy sweets at the house window on the Ashbury Lane side. They could also buy ice cream if they took a bowl to put it in.

Traction engine enthusiasts link the name of the firm Messrs J.G. & B. Earnshaw with the Allchin No. 3251 Royal Chester, built in 1925. By then the family lived at Gleadless. Elderly eyes still light up when mention is made of the Earnshaw brothers and their threshing machines!

JOHN EARNSHAW,

Traction Engine

— AND —

Thrashing Machine Proprietor

BLACKSMITH, WHEELWRIGHT, &c.

AGRICULTURAL IMPLEMENTS ATTENDED TO

DEALER IN DERBYSHIRE LIME
For Agricultural Purposes.

DEALER in SILKSTONE COAL DIRECT from COLLIERIES.

HEMSWORTH, NORTON

Near SHEFFIELD.

The grocery and off-licence shop, 246 Derbyshire Lane, in 1936. On the left is Thomas Joshua Davinson with a customer and Hetty Davinson, his daughter, on the right. The shop was destroyed by bombs in the Second World War and the site is now occupied by Derbyshire Lane Service Station. A hundred years ago, Mr Walter Cavill kept this shop. The road to the left is now called Cavill Road.

Margaret Dunn, probably at Whitsuntide 1936, near the cobbler's shop at 206 Derbyshire Lane owned by Benjamin Wilde. Note the advertisement on the side of the shop. Although only half of it is visible, many readers will be able to complete it as Cherry Blossom Boot Polish.

Mr Copley and his shop window display, c. 1910. Many of the brand names on the goods are still well-known today. Cocoa must have been a favourite drink, plus Bovril, Winox, ales and stout. In those days Harpic stated that its product 'Cleans the drains from house to mains.' What organization was offering the huge sum of £500 as a first prize? What is the significance of the cotton reel like object over the door?

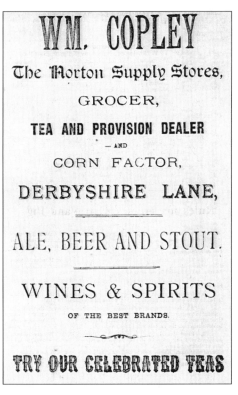

Mr Copley's shop was at 269 Derbyshire Lane, between Mount View Road and Harvey Clough Road. This advertisement dates from 1902.

WM. COPLEY

The Morton Supply Stores,

GROCER,

TEA AND PROVISION DEALER

— AND —

CORN FACTOR,

DERBYSHIRE LANE,

ALE, BEER AND STOUT.

WINES & SPIRITS

OF THE BEST BRANDS.

TRY OUR CELEBRATED TEAS

One of the papers sold at this Derbyshire Lane newsagent's was *The Jester*, published between 1882 and 1889.

These shops at the corner of Derbyshire Lane and Scarsdale Road include the one owned by Mrs E.M. Bell, whose name can just be seen over her shop. The surgery was set up here in the early 1950s by Dr Blake, who was soon joined by Dr Vivian.

In 1933, Mr J. Crann opened a fish shop on the corner of Meadow Head and Hunstone Avenue. The huge block of ice contains a large fish flanked by two Union flags and probably was in celebration of the Silver Jubilee of King George V in 1935. V. Crann is on the left, Evelyn, an assistant, is in the centre and a representative of Allen Senior, fish wholesaler of Grimsby, on the right.

Mr J. Crann's fish shop can just be seen on the right. Mr Crann bought the Elite Chocolate Box in 1939, just before the onset of war, in order to expand his business. Mr V. Crann added the greengrocery side of the business on the left hand side of this shop in 1959.

Newboult's garage at the corner of Meadowhead and Greenhill Main Road had a lot more character than the present modern one. Shell petrol is advertized on the ornate lanterns by the entrance and could be obtained for one shilling and a penny ha'penny a gallon (this is less than six modern pence). The Riley car owner may have just filled his tank with petrol from the tall cylindrical hand-worked pumps.

The first shops built next to Newboult's garage are listed in a 1934 directory as 364 Meadow Head, G.H. Gleadle, confectioner and 362 Meadow Head, G.H. Hill, grocer. The other shops in the row were completed by the following year.

Mitchell's shop at Meadowhead, opened in 1935. This picture was taken about 1955. Standing in front of the smart window display are Fred ?, John Mitchell and his mother Kathleen, Charlie Pearson and Dennis Mitchell. Some of us remember gratefully that Mr Mitchell campaigned to have the underpass built, after a Norton lady was run over near here.

The National Provincial Bank and other shops in the parade at Meadowhead top have changed hands several times since 1960. Percy Chapman's, electrical goods, cycles and toys, is now Barclays Bank. Mitchell is the only name still there, not selling meat but as a top-class wine merchant.

Tom Holmes & Sons, Builders, Bradway Road, photographed in 1980. Originally this was an old barn to the adjoining ancient farm. Tom Holmes took it over in about 1914 and he, and later his son, carried on the business until the late 1970s. It was bought by another building firm but soon closed and was then radically rebuilt to form this existing group of dwellings.

Numbers 50 to 56 Bradway Road, known for many years as Bowler's Cottages, in 1965. Mr Bowler started his Potted Meat Factory at the far end of the block about 1938. Before that it is believed to have been a laundry for Beauchief Hall and originally it may have been a Model Dairy for the Hall. The cottages are quite old, one having a date stone of 1760. They are now listed buildings.

The beer house on Bradway Lane in the early 1900s. It was known as the Miners' Arms until 1890-1900, then re-named The Bradway Hotel, later shortened to The Bradway. The railway tunnel diggers were known as miners, hence the initial name. It was completely re-built in the 1920s.

The Castle Inn, Bradway, at the end of a block of houses known as Castle Row, c. 1910. It started as a simple beer house to meet the demands of the 1,000 or more men constructing the Bradway Tunnel. An advertisement in 1866 stated that 'all that newly erected Beer House called the Castle Inn is to be let.'

The White Swan at Greenhill has been an inn for at least a century and a half. John Camm was the tenant in 1852. He was also a brick and tile maker, owning the quarry on Meadowhead. In 1902, as part of the Coronation celebrations, a dinner was given at the inn for sixty-four Greenhill men aged sixty or over. Entertainment was provided and packets of tea and tobacco were distributed to the veterans.

First Aid Post No. 26 was run by the ARP in the Second World War, in the old Greenhill School. Personnel on 30 June 1941 included Dr Wrench, centre front, with Mrs Wrench on his left. The lady second to the left of the doctor is Evelyn Thwaites.

Three firemen at Norton Fire Station during the Annual Inspection on 24 September 1954. From left to right: Mr Horsfield, Mr Brownbridge, Mr Knutton. Some firemen lived in pre-fabricated bungalows near the garages and workshops. The families contributed to the post-war life of Norton, younger children attending Norton Free School.

The Civil Defence used land near Jordanthorpe House during the Second World War. The No. 3 Norton Fire Station was established in the 1950s on the site of the present Church of the Latter Day Saints. At Christmas 1964 the last equipment was transferred to the new Low Edges fire station.

A group of Home Guard members from D Company, 65th West Riding Battalion, Norton during the Second World War. Lt Eastwood is standing on the left but names of the other men are not known. The main base was Norton House but they also met at the Transport Ground and at Hemsworth.

The presentation of a Scroll of Honour bearing the names of fifty four former members of C Company, 66th West Riding Battalion Home Guard, Old Comrades Association, 26 April 1959. This scroll is still in St James's church.

Seven
Our Goodly Heritage

St James's church, Norton, Parish Outing, c. 1900. The Revd G.W. Hall and Mrs Hall are at the centre back. Many outings were organised from the late 1880s to places as far afield as Southport, Morecambe, Cleethorpes and Bridlington, parishioners travelling by wagonettes and train. Local train travel became easier when the Dore and Totley tunnel was opened.

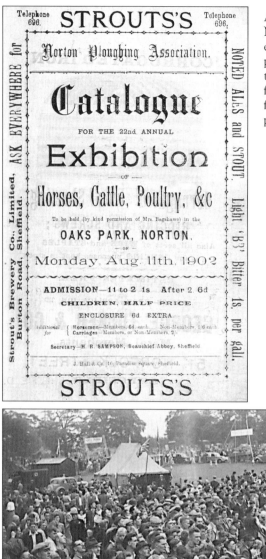

Agricultural shows held in the villages of North Derbyshire were a great source of entertainment and the farmers took great pride in their animals when exhibiting them. This 1902 catalogue cover gives a flavour of the activities; men on horseback, families in carriages and beer at five pence per gallon!

Something interesting was holding the attention of this large crowd at Norton Show. This photograph was taken in the fields by the Oakes, probably in the 1950s.

Margaret Elliott presenting a bouquet to Mrs Bagshawe of the Oakes at Norton Show in 1951. The other show officials are, from left to right: Mrs Elliott, Harold Glossop, Frank Bullifent and Levi Elliott.

In charge at Norton Show in 1951 are, from left to right: Arthur Gregory from Apperknowle, Levi Elliott of Hazelbarrow Farm, William Needham of Barlow Hall Farm, Ben Elliott of Hazelbarrow, Mr Crookes, Harold Glossop of Walkley, Secretary of Norton Ploughing Association and Mr Rose of Haslehurst Farm.

The Barlow Hunt Meet at the Oakes, Norton. Huntsman Spry is still remembered in Norton although he retired in 1951, nearly fifty years ago.

Presenting the stirrup cup at the Barlow Hunt Meet at the Oakes, Norton, in the 1940s. Standing on the left are William Haslam the terrier man, Sam Tomlinson from Ashover and the tall man is Major Wilson, the Master of the Hunt. The two ladies in the centre background (one with crutches) are Miss Violet and Miss May Wilson, twin sisters of the major. In the front, George Billam holds a jug and Harry Anderson the tray. Miss Elsie Wilson, the major's daughter, is mounted on the right.

The Barlow Hunt outside St James's church, Norton, another traditional meeting place for the Hunt.

Members of Norton Ploughing Association and Young Farmers' Club were present at the blessing of the plough on Plough Sunday at St James's, Norton, 10 Feb 1946. Mr Robinson of Dyche Lane Farm loaned the plough which was placed in the chancel during the service.

The ancient ceremony of the Boy Bishop was revived in 1949 in Norton and robes were specially made for the boys. The boy bishop preached a sermon, following the tradition established in Gloucester in 1558. Very few parishes had a boy bishop and Norton revived the tradition for only a few years. Norton's Boy Bishop in 1950 was Keith Bentley, on the right, and a visiting Boy Bishop from Mestycroft Wednesbury on the left. A colourful service was held in the church and the procession afterwards visited the Jessop Hospital Norton Annexe, formerly Norton Hall.

Outside the Jessop Hospital Norton Annexe after a Boy Bishop ceremony. The Bishop is Geoffrey Maynard with Christopher Barnes and Graham King as attendants and the Bishop's chaplain is David Walker. A member of the girls' choir is carrying the small processional cross.

Crowning of Norton's May Queen on the Vicarage Field (now Norton Church Glebe), *c.* 1950. Also present are the Queens of Greenhill and Bradway Sunday Schools, Canon Gledhill and members of the ladies' choir.

Sunday School Sports Day in the Vicarage Field, with the Rectory in the background.

A children's Peace Pageant took place in Sheffield on 17 July 1919 with the people of south Sheffield congregating in Meersbrook Park. According to the *Sheffield Independent*, processions left all the schools in the area and spectacular demonstrations were presented en route to the venue. At two-thirty in the afternoon all the assembly stood to attention while the *Last Post* was sounded in memory of those whose heroism had made peace celebrations possible. In each of four parks throughout the city a programme of hymns, national songs, physical exercise, games and dancing had been organised and at the Town Hall children gathered to present tableaux of Victory, Peace and Britannia. Mabel Rhodes from Norton was Britannia. After the celebrations, refreshments were provided at local schools and each scholar was provided with a medal. This was followed two days later by the Civic Celebration and March Past in Town Hall Square. Again, the tableaux were presented. *The Independent* reported 'These living pictures were a centre of much interest .... beautiful in their artistry, in their dainty dresses and in their show of English maidenhood.'

Norton Sunday School tea in the courtyard of the old Rectory in 1937, served by uniformed maids. The children from Bradway were conveyed by Mr Adlington's farm wagon and the smaller Greenhill children made the journey by courtesy of Mr Spittlehouse. All the children received a bag of sweets, the gift of Mr C. Richardson.

The Chantrey Award was created to celebrate the life and work of Sir Francis Chantrey. Children who lived in the ancient parish of Norton or who attended school in the area submitted drawings, paintings or clay models. The certificate was designed by G.R. Haith and a message was received from the Royal Academy wishing the venture every success. Lord John Manners presented the prizes and certificates at the first Award ceremony on 12 July 1952.

Norton Association
for the Prosecution of Felons.

Established at Mr. Joseph Broomhead's, The Bowling Green, Maugerhay, Jan. 1st, 1784

President - Mr. P. B. DAVIDSON.

Vice-President:	Solicitor:	Treasurer:	Secretary:
Mr. G. FIELDING.	Mr. R. J. FLETCHER.	Mr. H. ETCHELLS.	Mr. F. E. SLATER.

Tel. 72566.

9, Dewar Drive,
Sheffield, 7.
26th February, 1952

Dear Sir,

The ONE HUNDRED AND SIXTY-FIRST

ANNUAL MEETING & DINNER

of the above Association, will be held at the **Bagshawe Arms, Norton, on Wednesday, 12th March, 1952, at 6.30 p.m. prompt.**

I shall be obliged if you will kindly return the attached slip not later than March 4th, so that arrangements can be made with the caterer.

It is hoped that members will bring as many friends as they can to this function who will automatically become full members of the Association for the current year.

Male members of the Young Farmers' Club aged 18 or over will be accepted as members at the reduced subscription of 7/6 (including dinner).

Yours faithfully,
F. E. SLATER, Secretary.

Annual Subscription, 10/- (which includes cost of Dinner).

The Norton Association for the Prosecution of Felons and Receivers of Stolen Goods and Cattle and other Legal Objects was established at Mr Joseph Broomhead's, the Bowling Green, Maugerhay on 1 January 1784. The rules state that the Annual General Meeting shall be held during the first three months of the year, on a day of the week nearest full moon, and at such meeting members shall dine together.

Members of Holmhirst Road Methodist church on Whit Monday 1954 assembling their procession before walking around the local district.

Glenda Houghton, the Holmhirst Road Methodist church Sunday School Queen of 1955 and the Captain, M. Porter, processing along Chesterfield Road, passing Helmton Road corner. The shop on the right is now Williams of Woodseats.

Couples who had been married in St James's were invited by the Revd M. Williams to attend a Valentine's Service of thanksgiving in 1978. The Bishop of Doncaster, the Rt Revd Stuart Cross preached the sermon. Arthur and Maggie Bashforth, who were married forty-seven years previously, travelled from Thirsk to renew their marriage vows.

Miss Muriel Bagshawe of the Oakes-in-Norton married Mr Bradshaw-Isherwood in November 1907. When they returned from honeymoon in December they were welcomed home by this magnificent arch, made by the villagers and decorated with flags, foliage and chinese lanterns. Neighbours, friends, tenants and employees gathered at the Oakes for a big celebration.

112

Eight
Home and Away

Bradway Cricket Club, *c.* 1912. The club used a ground situated between the present day Evangelical Church and Edmund Avenue. The wicket seems to have been roughly where the centre white line of Greenhill Parkway is today. The wooden hut was the pavilion, the stone cottage to its left was Mundy's cobbler's shop from 1925, the two cottages in the centre still exist, as do the houses in the background on Bradway Road.

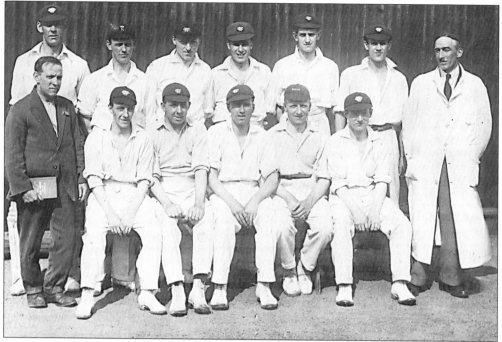

Norton Woodseats is an old-established cricket club still playing in Graves Park. The club First XI won the Norton and District Cricket League in 1929. From left to right, back row: T. Wainwright, T. Cork, A. Holmes, J. Richardson, R. Helliwell, H. Helliwell, A. Rhodes (umpire). Front row: G. Hulme (scorer), D. Adcock, V. Whittington, G. Richardson (captain), P. Rose, F. May.

Norton Woodseats Cricket Club XI, Sheffield League, A Division Winners 1958. From left to right, back row: B. Farmer, D. Salt, D. Chattle, I. Bronks, B. Cousins, R. Roberts. Front row: K. Hill, B. Richardson, K. Littlewood, A. Cousins, B. Ledger.

Footballers in front of the Bradway Cricket Club pavilion, c. 1922. The team contained: D. Mundy, Bert Howe, H. Arnould, C. Belbin, J. Hill, B. Rudd, J. Coffey, W. Guard, B. Arnould, Reg Cox, J. Harrop and L. Arnould.

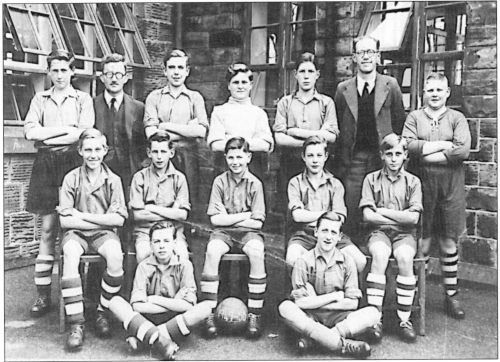

Greenhill School Football XI members in 1949-50 From left to right, back row: Gerald Holmes, Mr Sowerby (headmaster), Brian Green, Douglas Ridgway, Roy Hackett, Mr G. Walker (teacher), John Ellis. Middle row: Keith Maddocks, Brian Elston, Tony Bingham, Peter Hampson, Michael Ambler. Front row: Tony Ellis and Roy Ellis.

This fine boathouse with a thatched roof was beside the lower lake in Graves Park. The lake became crowded with water lilies in the late 1970s and funding was not available for repairs to the boats, so this leisure activity had to be discontinued.

Graves Park has three lakes connected by a stream originating near Bunting Nook. The top lake is a wild-life sanctuary, the middle lake is reserved for fishing and the lower lake was used for boating.

An open air theatre was the scene of many successful productions and two of these shows, in 1944 and 1945, were repeated in the City Hall.

The theatre occupied a site in Graves Park, bordering Meadowhead (A61) and opposite a former quarry and brickworks which is now the site of a Safeway supermarket.

Mrs Annie Hall enjoying a picnic in the Moss Valley sometime near the beginning of the twentieth century.

This late nineteenth-century photograph shows Revd G.W. Hall, a keen angler, standing at the door to the parish library, a large room in the Rectory.

Miss Pegge, daughter of the Revd J.S. Pegge, giving a ride to John Robinson in the Rectory yard in 1938. John lived in Norton Green Lodge, now the site of Norton Lawns, at the corner of Norton Lane and School Lane.

Louise Hanwell and Philip Wetherill riding Solomon, at Chantrey House, Maugerhay, in 1959.

A group of Norton ladies enjoying an outing in 1928.

The Norton Church Women's Fellowship members, shown here with Canon Gledhill in 1960, include Beryl Wright, Jean Dewsnap, Irene Shaw, Mrs Gledhill, Barbara Hall, Ellie Turney, Win Peters, Dorothy Wilkinson, Kath White, Betty Marsden, Barbara Wheelhouse, Win Wild, Dorrie McCreery, Pat Locke and Ruth Harris.

THIS REPRESENTS

A SHARE

IN THE YOUTH WORK IN THE

PARISH OF NORTON

Your gift has helped to build the Youth Hall in
the Rectory field. You will be fully repaid in the
happiness your gift will bring to succeeding
generations of Youth using this hall.

NORTON PARISH CHURCH · 1956

One thousand shares of ten shillings each were issued to raise the deficit of £500 to complete
the building of the Youth Hall. Grants were received from the Ministry of Education and the
Sheffield Council of Boys' Clubs. There was also a house to house collection in the Norton
area, as well as concerts and whist drives. The design of the pelican feeding its young echoes
that in the east window of the Blythe Chapel in Norton church.

Guides and Scouts at a Church Parade at St James's Norton, *c.* 1960. Included in the photograph are Elizabeth Schofield, Ann Bawd, Elizabeth Stuart-King, Ann Humphrey and Peter Shaw.

Putting the finishing touches to a mural in Norton Church Youth Hall in 1958. Stan Dickinson, youth leader, is on the left.

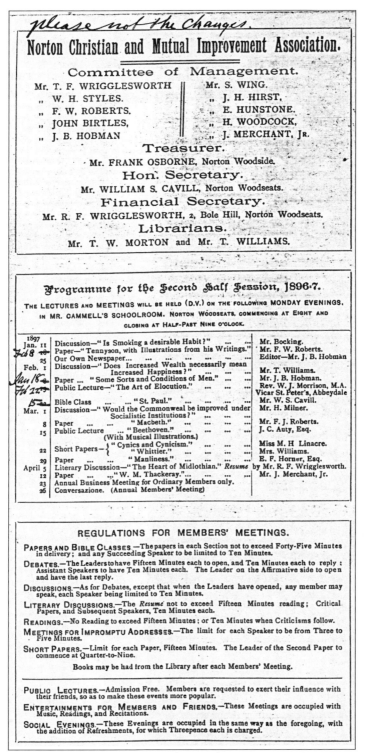

please not the changes.

Norton Christian and Mutual Improvement Association.

Committee of Management.

Mr. T. F. WRIGGLESWORTH	Mr. S. WING.
„ W. H. STYLES.	„ J. H. HIRST.
„ F. W. ROBERTS.	„ E. HUNSTONE.
„ JOHN BIRTLES,	„ H. WOODCOCK,
„ J. B. HOBMAN	„ J. MERCHANT, JR.

Treasurer.
Mr. FRANK OSBORNE, Norton Woodside.

Hon. Secretary.
Mr. WILLIAM S. CAVILL, Norton Woodseats.

Financial Secretary.
Mr. R. F. WRIGGLESWORTH, 2, Bole Hill, Norton Woodseats.

Librarians.
Mr. T. W. MORTON and Mr. T. WILLIAMS.

Programme for the Second Half Session, 1896-7.

THE LECTURES AND MEETINGS WILL BE HELD (D.V.) ON THE FOLLOWING MONDAY EVENINGS, IN MR. CAMMELL'S SCHOOLROOM. NORTON WOODSEATS. COMMENCING AT EIGHT AND CLOSING AT HALF-PAST NINE O'CLOCK.

1897		
Jan. 11	Discussion—" Is Smoking a desirable Habit?"	Mr. Bocking.
Feb 8	Paper—" Tennyson, with Illustrations from his Writings."	Mr. F. W. Roberts.
25	Our Own Newspaper...	Editor—Mr. J. B. Hobman
Feb. 1	Discussion—" Does Increased Wealth necessarily mean Increased Happiness?"	Mr. T. Williams.
Jan 18	Paper ... " Some Sorts and Conditions of Men."	Mr. J. B. Hobman.
Feb 22	Public Lecture—" The Art of Elocution."	Rev. W. J. Morrison, M.A. Vicar St. Peter's, Abbeydale.
15	Bible Class ... ... " St. Paul."	Mr. W. S. Cavill.
Mar. 1	Discussion—" Would the Commonweal be improved under Socialistic Institutions?"	Mr. H. Milner.
8	Paper ... ... " Macbeth."	Mr. F. J. Roberts.
15	Public Lecture ... " Beethoven." (With Musical Illustrations.)	J. C. Auty, Esq.
22	Short Papers— { " Cynics and Cynicism."	Miss M. H Linacre.
	{ " Whittier."	Mrs. Williams.
29	Paper ... ... " Manliness."	E. F. Horner, Esq.
April 5	Literary Discussion—" The Heart of Midlothian." *Resumé* by Mr. R. F. Wrigglesworth.	
12	Paper ... ..." W. M. Thackeray."...	Mr. J. Merchant, Jr.
23	Annual Business Meeting for Ordinary Members only.	
26	Conversazione. (Annual Members' Meeting)	

REGULATIONS FOR MEMBERS' MEETINGS.

PAPERS AND BIBLE CLASSES.—The papers in each Section not to exceed Forty-Five Minutes in delivery; and any Succeeding Speaker to be limited to Ten Minutes.

DEBATES.—The Leaders to have Fifteen Minutes each to open, and Ten Minutes each to reply : Assistant Speakers to have Ten Minutes each. The Leader on the Affirmative side to open and have the last reply.

DISCUSSIONS.—As for Debates, except that when the Leaders have opened, any member may speak, each Speaker being limited to Ten Minutes.

LITERARY DISCUSSIONS.—The *Resumé* not to exceed Fifteen Minutes reading; Critical Papers, and Subsequent Papers, Ten Minutes each.

READINGS.—No Reading to exceed Fifteen Minutes ; or Ten Minutes when Criticisms follow.

MEETINGS FOR IMPROMPTU ADDRESSES.—The limit for each Speaker to be from Three to Five Minutes.

SHORT PAPERS.—Limit for each Paper, Fifteen Minutes. The Leader of the Second Paper to commence at Quarter-to-Nine.

Books may be had from the Library after each Members' Meeting.

PUBLIC LECTURES.—Admission Free. Members are requested to exert their influence with their friends, so as to make these events more popular.

ENTERTAINMENTS FOR MEMBERS AND FRIENDS,—These Meetings are occupied with Music, Readings, and Recitations.

SOCIAL EVENINGS.—These Evenings are occupied in the same way as the foregoing, with the addition of Refreshments, for which Threepence each is charged.

The programme for Norton Christian and Mutual Improvement Association in 1897.

Stan and Margaret Gascoigne of Greenhill on their very heavy Claud Butler tandem. It had been lovingly stored by its owner throughout the Second World War and sold to them in 1948. Stan was also a racing cyclist and was a member of the 'possibles' squad for the 1948 Olympics but then a bad crash ended all ambition of riding for his country.

Mr and Mrs Dunn of Derbyshire Lane had a motor-cycle and side-car in the 1930s. Their children still have happy memories of days out in the country and at the seaside.

Few people owned a car in the 1930s. Samuel and Harriett Bishop are seen here motoring in Woodseats in their smart two-seater.

By 1958 more cars were on the road. It was great fun to work out how to pack all the summer holiday gear. This is Pat Shipton, her brother Frank and their Dad, outside their Derbyshire Lane house at Four Lane Ends.

Sheffield manufacturers of special alloy steels, used in the manufacture of aircraft engines, raised money in 1916 to buy an aeroplane for presentation to the Dominion of Newfoundland in the name of Sheffield. The Master Cutler, W.H. Ellis, and the Mistress Cutler handed over the aircraft to Lord Hugh Cecil at the First World War landing field at Jordanthorpe (Coal Aston). Thousands of people watched a flying display by the new machine.

Here is an Avro 504K aircraft at Norton in July 1932, the first year when National Aviation Day Displays took place. Sir Alan Cobham and E.B. Fielden of Aviation Tours took an array of aircraft round the country and many Norton residents were thrilled to have the chance to take a first short flight.

Another aircraft at Norton in 1932 was G-EBBI, a Handley Page W8b which could accommodate ten passengers in some comfort. It was made in 1922, used by Imperial Airways from 1924 to 1931 and scrapped in October 1932. During the First World War the hangar in the background was part of the No.2 (Northern) Aircraft Repair Depot. Pilots collected repaired aircraft from the hangar and then took off from the adjacent field. It is now the site of the Graves Tennis Centre.

The kettle was on the hob and it was time for a cuppa for Mr Herbert Morton, the farmer at Mansion House Farm in 1958. This wonderful range was highly regarded because, in addition to the obvious cooking and drying facilities, a plentiful supply of hot water could be drawn from the tap on the left.

Mr Herbert Morton, on the left, taking time off for a rest in his kitchen at Mansion House Farm, Lightwood Lane. His visitor was Mr Davenport of Coal Aston, who dropped in occasionally for a cup of tea and a chat.